ACADIA FIELD GUIDE

A Guided Tour of Acadia's Park Loop Road

TravelBrains®

Travel adventures that leave you smarter!

ACADIA FIELD GUIDE
A guided tour of Acadia's Park Loop Road
ISBN 1-933763-01-9

Dedicated to the "Thin Green Line"
America's park rangers

TravelBrains would like to thank the following individuals and institutions for their contributions to the Acadia Field Guide. Your help was greatly appreciated.

Deborah Dyer
Dani Fazio
Chris Havern
Robert G. Marvinney, Ph.D.
John McDade
Laurie Olson
Tom Patterson
Joyce Peterson
Deborah Wade

National Park Service
Bar Harbor Historical Association
Maine Historical Society
Maine Geological Survey
United States Geological Survey
United States Coast Guard

CORPORATE SALES
Companies, institutions and other organizations wishing to make bulk purchases of this or any other TravelBrains products should contact the sales department toll-free at (888) 458-6475 or email us at info@travelbrains.com. We are also available online at www.TravelBrains.com.

DISCLAIMER
This book is intended for viewing at tour stops only. Please keep your eyes on the road at all times while driving. TravelBrains shall have neither liability nor responsibility to any person or entity with respect to any loss or damage caused, or alleged to have been caused, directly or indirectly, by the use of this product. Acadia is a beautiful, but also inherently dangerous place. TravelBrains has attempted to warn readers of all potential dangers. However, TravelBrains assumes no liability for accidents or injuries incurred by readers who engage in any of the activities described in this book or audio tour.

Printed in Malaysia

CONTENTS

Ellsworth

15
172

3

1

West Gouldsboro

Gouldsboro

186
195

186

Winter Harbor

Blue Hill

15

Mount
Desert
Island

Bar
Harbor

3

Park Loop Road

Schoodic
Peninsula

102

*Acadia
National
Park*

Southwest
Harbor

Northeast
Harbor

Deer
Isle

Bass Harbor

Stonington

Swans
Island

Isle au Haut

ACADIA NATIONAL PARK

Acadia National Park consists of a patchwork of properties along the Maine coast. Most of Acadia is located on Mount Desert Island, the second-largest island on the east coast of the United States. The park also includes parcels of land on Isle au Haut, a remote island about 15 miles southwest of Mount Desert Island, and on Schoodic Peninsula, the only mainland section of the park. Acadia was the first National Park east of the Mississippi and the only one created entirely from donated private property.

This tour will take you along Acadia's Park Loop Road, a spectacular 27-mile circuit that passes many of Acadia's highlights, from Sand Beach to Thunder Hole to Cadillac Mountain. Each tour stop has its own audio track. After you listen to the introduction on audio track one, simply drive to the tour stop you wish to visit and play the audio track number associated with it.

As you tour the park, please remember to leave no trace by walking on designated paths, taking only pictures, and leaving all rocks and creatures where you find them.

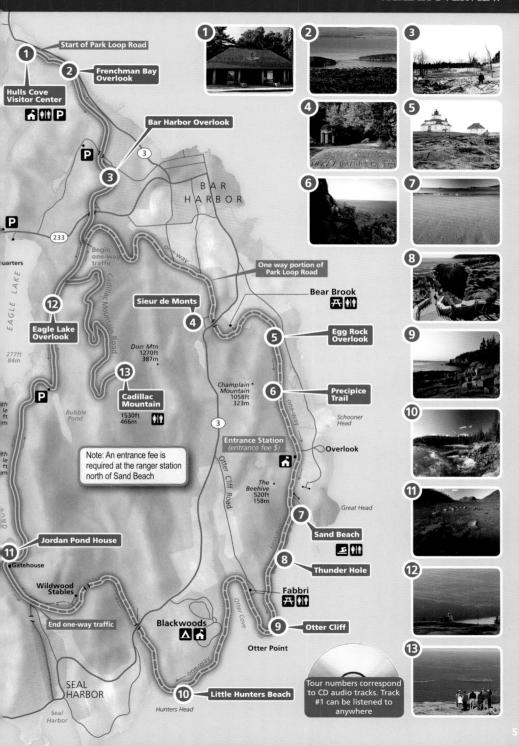

Start of Park Loop Road

Frenchman Bay Overlook

Hulls Cove Visitor Center

Bar Harbor Overlook

BAR HARBOR

Begin one-way traffic

One way portion of Park Loop Road

Bear Brook

Sieur de Monts

Egg Rock Overlook

Eagle Lake Overlook

Dorr Mtn 1270ft 387m

Champlain Mountain 1058ft 323m

Precipice Trail

Cadillac Mountain 1530ft 466m

Schooner Head

Entrance Station (entrance fee $)

Overlook

Note: An entrance fee is required at the ranger station north of Sand Beach

The Beehive 520ft 158m

Great Head

Jordan Pond House

Gatehouse

Sand Beach

Wildwood Stables

Thunder Hole

Fabbri

End one-way traffic

Blackwoods

Otter Cliff

Otter Point

SEAL HARBOR

Little Hunters Beach

Hunters Head

Seal Harbor

EAGLE LAKE

277ft 84m

Quarters

Cadillac Mountain Road

Bubble Pond

Otter Cliff Road

Otter Cove

Tour numbers correspond to CD audio tracks. Track #1 can be listened to anywhere

5

GEOLOGY OVERVIEW

There are several different rock formations that helped form Acadia National Park. Its oldest rocks started off at the bottom of the ocean approximately 500 million years ago. Heat, pressure, and time transformed the sea floor into *metamorphic* rock that was eventually pushed to the surface by colliding tectonic plates. Today, that ancient seabed is called the Ellsworth Schist. Evidence of it can be seen in the northwest section of the island.

Another ancient seabed that became *sedimentary* rock can be seen around Bar Harbor, and a third rock formation resulted from volcanic eruptions that spewed hot molten material into the sea. The resulting *igneous* rock can be seen on the southwestern side of the island and the Cranberry Isles. All three of these rock formations play second fiddle, however, to the main attraction among the rock formations at Acadia National Park. Pink granite is the star of the show.

Granite, a form of igneous rock, is the most abundant type of rock on the island and forms the mountains that dominate Acadia's topography. All granite is born of molten rock that cooled and hardened underneath the surface of the Earth. Here in Acadia, the granite that composes the bulk of the island formed millions of years ago, when a plume of magma bubbled up from the Earth's core and slowly cooled as it approached the surface.

As the pool of magma pushed its way upward, it melted and fractured the rock above it. Chunks of the older rock mixed with the newer granite, creating a chocolate chip cookie dough-like appearance in places. Geologists call this area of contact the *shatter zone*. You can find evidence of it in places like Otter Point, Great Head, and Little Hunters Beach.

The word granite is derived from the Latin word *granum*, meaning "grain." If you take a

A plume of magma slowly cools near the Earth's surface, forming granite.

Fragments of the older bedrock break off and are absorbed by the magma, forming what will become the shatter zone.

close look at granite, you will notice that it is composed of a grainy pattern of crystals. The size of the crystals is related to how quickly the magma cools: the slower the cooling, the larger the crystals. Granite with large, thumb-sized crystals comes from deep within the Earth, while granite with small, rice-sized crystals forms much closer to the surface.

There are several different types of granite on the island that can be classified by their mineral content, coloration, and crystal size. Perhaps the most distinctive of all is Cadillac Mountain granite. Its pink color comes from the feldspar crystals that dominate the rock. The next most prominent mineral in Cadillac Mountain granite is clear-colored quartz. The small dark crystals are hornblende.

Hornblende is the first mineral to crystallize during the cooling process. Unconstrained by other minerals, it forms the most perfectly shaped crystals. It is the feldspar and quartz, however, that endow granite with its legendary hardness. That ruggedness helps explain how Acadia's granite, which formed underground, found its way to the surface. Millions of years of rain, glaciers, rivers and surf eventually stripped away the weaker rocks resting above it, leaving behind the solid granite domes and chiseled shoreline that are the hallmarks of Acadia today.

The mineral feldspar gives Acadia's granite a pink hue. The light colored mineral is quartz and the black crystals are hornblende.

Evidence of the shatter zone can be found on the periphery of the former magma plume.

Millions of years of erosion stripped away the weaker bedrock that rested atop the granite, revealing Acadia's granite domes and shoreline.

GLACIERS

Glaciers have done more than any other force to mold the park's modern-day features. Evidence of these massive ice sheets can be found everywhere in the park, from enormous boulders perched on the tops of mountains to classic U-shaped valleys.

Glaciers show up in Acadia on a remarkably regular basis. During the last million years, this area has experienced approximately eight glaciations. Each glacial period lasts approximately 100,000 years. In between these long cold stretches, the Earth warms up for about 10,000 years. Then things cool down and we start the process all over again. Currently we're in the middle of one of these interglacial periods. In all likelihood, Acadia will return to its usual frozen state - fortunately for us, probably not for another several thousand years from now.

During the last glacial period in this region, the Laurentide Ice Sheet advanced south through Maine and extended over 300 miles out to sea. This solid body of ice, 1-2 miles thick, stretched across most of Canada, reaching as far south as New York and Chicago. The weight of it literally depressed the surface of the Earth.

When the southbound glacier reached Acadia, it ran into a granite ridge that ran roughly east-west. In some places, the glacier dug troughs through the rock along a north-south axis. Technically called *glacial notches*, the U-shaped valleys you see today in places like Bubble Pond and Jordan Pond are the carved out remains of glacier pathways.

In other locations, the ice was forced up over the ridge. The resulting pressure produced a thin layer of meltwater that the glacier rode up to the top. When the ice crested the mountain, the pressure was released and the water refroze, taking hold in any nooks and crannies. As the glacier continued its journey, the icy fingers ripped or plucked chunks of rock off the descending portion of the mountain and carried them away. Geologists call this process *glacial plucking*. Good examples of it can be found at the Beehive and South Bubble Mountain.

Geologists also study the surface of granite in Acadia for clues to what the ice was transporting. If the ice was carrying large amounts of clay and silt, the glaciers acted like sandpaper and literally polished the granite smooth. You can find evidence of *glacial polish* in Acadia near the Tarn and Great Head.

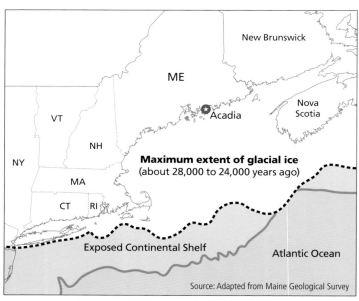

During the last glacial period, the Laurentide Ice Sheet advanced south through Maine and extended over 300 miles out to sea.

Sometimes the glaciers dragged large rocks across the surface. If the rock was dragged in a continuous fashion it left long narrow scratches in the surface called *striations*. If the boulder was repeatedly pushed into the bedrock, it left a series of crescent shaped depressions called *chatter marks* where the stone pivoted and shifted until it was free to move with the glacier again.

When the glaciers finally melted, the boulders and rocks that were being swept along with the flow of ice were left stranded far from their previous homes. These transplanted boulders are called *glacial erratics*. You can find them all over the island, but the most famous one in Acadia is Bubble Rock, perched on the summit of South Bubble Mountain. In some locations, the glacier left behind a pile of rocks and debris called a *moraine*. The Jordan Pond House sits on a moraine that acted as a natural dam, helping create Jordan Pond.

When the weight of all that ice was removed, the ground began to rise. This is known as *post-glacial rebound*. Prior to the rebound though, the oceans began filling with water from melting glaciers, drowning the depressed land in eastern Maine. At one point, some 13,000 years ago, the sea was crashing on a shoreline that was as much as 300 feet above today's sea level. Evidence of the ancient shoreline can be seen on some of Acadia's hiking trails.

When the land eventually began to rise, it actually outpaced the rising water for a period. The result was just as strange to witness: large portions of the sea floor rose out of the water. Many parts of Frenchman Bay were high and dry and Mount Desert Island wasn't even an island anymore - it was part of the mainland. Over time, water continued to fill the oceans and sea levels eventually reached their present states.

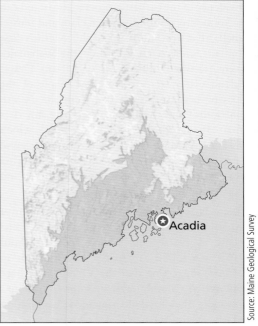

Source: Maine Geological Survey

13,000 Years ago, before the Earth's crust had rebounded from the weight of the glaciers, a large portion of Maine was below sea level.

RELATIVE LAND AND SEA LEVELS

Present land and sea levels

Relative Land and sea levels

Land-level curve

Emerged land

Sea-level curve

Drowned coast

Time

Start of glacial cycle

Maximum glaciation

Present

Source: Adapted from Maine Geological Survey

Maine's coastline has seen dramatic changes, as the land rebounded from the previous Ice Age, and melting glaciers filled the oceans.

A BRIEF HISTORY OF ACADIA

Evidence of the earliest visitors to the island can be found in piles of discarded clam and mussel shells that are 6,000 years old. Maine's first Indians, collectively known as the Wabanaki, were transient inhabitants of Mount Desert Island. They were called the "People of the Dawn" because they hailed from the eastern portion of the continent, where the sun rises first. They called the island Pemetic, which meant "mountain range" and they made good use of the island's natural resources, hunting for seals from birch bark canoes, fishing, and collecting mussels and clams.

There is some debate among historians over when Europeans first visited the Maine coast. A Norse coin dating back to about 1070 was found at a native encampment in Maine, suggesting that the Vikings may have discovered Maine even before Columbus's voyage. The first documented exploration of the Maine coast by a European was led by Giovanni da Verrazzano in 1524. He was searching for a passage to Asia and ended up exploring the east coast of what is now the United States.

Later, in the mid 1500s, a tale of a city of gold named Norumbega, thought to exist up one of the larger rivers in what is now Maine, spurred a series of expeditions in search of the treasure. However, no gold was ever found and Maine remained unsettled by Europeans through the end of the century.

In 1603, King Henry IV of France granted Pierre Dugua, a French nobleman, the rights to all the fur trade in the New World and placed all the land stretching roughly from present day Philadelphia to Cape Breton under his control. Intent on establishing an outpost and exploring his territory, Dugua recruited an expedition force that included a navigator named Samuel de Champlain. When Champlain saw the bare summits of the island's mountains he wrote in his diary:

"The island is very high and notched in places, so that there is the appearance to one at sea, as of seven or eight mountains extending along near each other. The summit of most of them is destitute of trees, as there are only rocks on them...I named it L'isle des Monts-Desert."

The name Mount Desert – or "Island of Barren Mountains" - stuck. But the French were unable to hold the territory, losing it to the British during the French and Indian War. After the conflict was over, English settlers moved in. By 1796, Revolutionary hero Samuel Adams, then governor of Massachusetts (which at the time included present-day Maine), signed the papers that incorporated Eden, Mount Desert Island's second town. Eden, which would later become Bar Harbor, was a hardscrabble outpost where islanders fished, built ships,

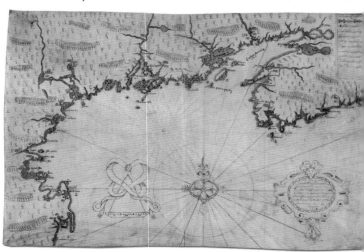

Champlain's map of the New World

cultivated crops, and logged the woods, like so many other Mainers.

Then, in 1844 something happened that would change the island forever: the nation's preeminent landscape painter, Thomas Cole, showed up with his palette and an easel. In this time before photography, paintings by Cole and other prominent artists of the famed Hudson River School of Art drew tourists to the island from all over. Champlain may have named the island, but it was these artists who put it on the map.

Soon intellectuals and other elites who had the money and time to make the multi-day journey were exploring Mount Desert Island. These early tourists were called *Rusticators* because they came for the simple pleasures the island had

Samuel de Champlain

to offer, staying in modest accommodations, often in the homes of locals. As more tourists arrived, hotels began sprouting like dandelions – there were 30 by 1880. The Rodick House hotel in Bar Harbor boasted over 600 rooms and claimed to be the largest hotel in Maine. But hotels weren't quite sufficient for families like the Rockefellers, Morgans, Carnegies, and Vanderbilts. Wealth like that needed more exclusive accommodations. So they built palatial summer homes, called their 80-room mansions "cottages," and moved "Down East" every July. Soon Bar Harbor was *the* place to be in the summertime.

The rapid pace of development dismayed many who wished to preserve the island's natural beauty. Lead by a man named George Dorr, these concerned individuals began a conservation movement that would eventually result in Acadia National Park. The efforts of men like Dorr, Charles Eliot, and John D. Rockefeller Jr. were eventually rewarded in 1916 when President Wilson designated the area as a national monument. Congress would later make it a national park, the first one east of the Mississippi, and the first national park comprised entirely of donated lands.

Thomas Cole's painting of Frenchman Bay during a squall

THOMAS COLE

Born in Bolton, England, in 1801, Thomas Cole was America's foremost landscape painter when he arrived at Mount Desert in 1844. His passion for the island was shared by one of his student prodigies, Frederic Church. Both painters were members of the Hudson River School of Art, an artistic movement that sought to shift the public's perception of the wilderness from something that needed to be conquered and tamed, to something with intrinsic value, worth preserving. Their paintings of Mount Desert Island were exhibited in cities across the country and sparked a boom in tourism that hasn't let up yet. Their paintings also helped fuel a conservation movement which ultimately helped produce Acadia National Park.

FRENCHMAN BAY

Though it's hard to believe, this great basin was once largely dry. During the last Ice Age, a period called the Wisconsin Glaciation, sheets of ice the size of continents pressed down on this part of Maine. The weight of the ice caused a depression in Earth's crust. Then, about 18,000 years ago, the climate became warmer. The retreating glaciers relieved the land of its heavy burden and the land began to rise. Around 11,000 years ago Mount Desert Island wasn't even an island - it was part of the mainland. Eventually, the melting glaciers filled the oceans and sea levels reached their modern levels, resulting in the bay you see today.

Many historians believe the bay takes its name from the French warships that used the many islands of the bay as cover to launch attacks on the British, back when the English and French wrestled for control of this region. Islands like Ironbound, Stave, and Bar were perfect for concealing their tall frigates.

At low tide, the gravel bar connecting Bar Island with th

Frenchman Bay

Lead Mountain

Schoodic Mountains

Gouldsboro Hills

Bar Island

Bar Harb

Calf Island

Frenchman Bay seen from Cadillac Mountain

THE PORCUPINE ISLANDS

The Porcupine Islands are so named because of the piny evergreens that poke up off their backs toward the sky. Or are they? According to the native Wabanaki, these four small isles were once porcupines that lived on Cadillac Mountain as the pets of an angry giant. One night the prickly quartet was creating quite a ruckus as their keeper was sleeping. The giant flew into a rage and chased them down into the bay. There, a mermaid came to their aid and quickly changed them into islands so they would be safe from the giant forever.

Harbor is exposed.

Sheep Porcupine Island

Burnt Porcupine Island

Stave Island

Long Porcupine Island

Bald Porcupine Island

Jordan Island

Ironbound Island

MILLIONAIRE'S ROW

At the dawn of the twentieth century, there was no place more fashionable to be in the summer than Bar Harbor, Maine. One writer described the community as the "unchallengeable queen of Eastern summer-resorts." From the Rockefellers to the Astors to the Vanderbilts, many of the most prominent and affluent families in the nation built summer homes along the shore here. They hired the country's fanciest architects to design them 80-room "cottages," and then moved up for the months of July and August, when the heat of the city became unbearable. Wingwood (pictured above), for example, was owned by a senior partner from JP Morgan. It boasted 80 rooms, 26 hand-carved marble fireplaces, 28 bathrooms, some with gold fixtures, 52 telephone lines, and an entire wing of 30 rooms for the servants.

Wingwood

By the 1890s, there were more than 175 of these mansions. If you drove a carriage along present day Route 3 on the way into town you would have seen one after another lined up along what was known then as Millionaire's Row.

For social clubs and servants and soirées – Bar Harbor was unmatched. This was a world of parties and privilege, drivers and servants, croquet on the lawn and soirées into the wee hours.

Courtesy of Jesup Memorial Libr

THE FIRE OF 47

On October 24, 1947, the Bangor Daily News read: "Thousands Flee as Raging Blaze Sweeps Bar Harbor: Famed Resort Feared Doomed." That summer had been one of the driest on record with no substantial rain in 108 days. By late October, much of Maine was ready to burn. And on one fine Indian Summer day, a Bar Harbor woman reported that she had seen smoke at the local dump. No one's sure what kindled it. The flames smoldered for a few days, but on the fourth day it was picked up by winds and spread quickly, growing in intensity each day. Things got really ugly on October 23, when gale force winds turned the full force of the blaze in the direction of Bar Harbor.

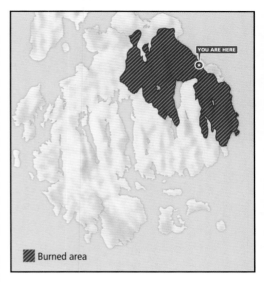

Burned area

The inferno cut a three-mile-wide swath toward the resort town, consuming everything in its path, including houses and businesses. Residents tried to flee but found themselves walled in by flames, and many went to the town pier to await rescue by sea. Fishermen evacuated 400 by boat but thousands more were still trapped.

Crews from the Army, the Coast Guard, the National Park Service, local colleges, and even the Bangor Theological Seminary poured in to help contain the great conflagration. They couldn't save the vast estates of Millionaire's Row, Jackson Laboratory, and many other businesses along Route 3. But a crew was able to push through the flames with a bulldozer to clear a path for the evacuation. A parade of 700 cars, carrying 2,000 people, drove off the island, flames licking, and sparks landing on their roofs as they went. The main part of the blaze burned all the way to Great Head Peninsula before exploding out over the sea, but other little fires continued to burn until November 14.

By the end of the fire more than 17,000 acres went up in flames. Five deaths were attributed to the fire and more than 170 year-round homes were lost, including almost all of the wealthy cottages in Bar Harbor and five historic hotels. Damage exceeded $23 million dollars – the equivalent of $286 million today.

SIEUR DE MONTS SPRING

Sieur de Monts Spring was named after the French nobleman, Pierre Dugua, who was given the rights to everything between the 40th and 46th parallel by the king of France back in 1603. That's approximately everything from Pennsylvania up to Nova Scotia. Sieur de Mons was Pierre Dugua's noble title. When Dugua set sail to colonize the New World, he hired Samuel Champlain to be his navigator. Champlain, as you will recall, is the man who gave Mount Desert Island its name.

In 1909, George Dorr constructed the octagonal well cover over the spring. He thought the waters here were so pure he had "Sweet Waters of Acadia" inscribed on a boulder beside the pond, a reference to the "Sweet Waters of Europe" and "Sweet Waters of Asia," springs that he had seen on his travels to Constantinople.

Dorr donated the spring and adjacent land to help preserve Mount Desert Island for future generations. His efforts would ultimately lead to the creation of Acadia National Park. Sieur de Monts spring is a fitting memorial to the man who was described as "the greatest of one-man shows in the history of land conservation."

The mountain that sits behind the spring was originally called Flying Squadron Mountain. After Dorr's death, it was renamed Dorr Mountain in his honor. The path that runs behind the spring leads to a trail with a steep climb up to the summit.

SIEUR DE MONT FACILITIES

At Sieur de Monts Springs you'll discover Acadia's Nature Center, the Wild Gardens of Acadia, a branch of the Abbe Museum, and several hiking trails trundling up adjacent mountains. The Nature Center offers a great opportunity to see what the park's interpretive rangers and biologists are up to. Inside are displays that document the various research programs actively being pursued at Acadia.

On the grounds, the gardeners of the Wild Gardens of Acadia have recreated a dozen of the plant communities you'll find across the island, from mixed woods to seaside to mountain. All of these are situated on less than an acre and are explored by pleasant trails with self-guided interpretation.

The Abbe Museum is a small collection of native artifacts that is part of the larger Abbe Museum in Bar Harbor. It showcases the antique Native treasures amassed by Dr. Robert Abbe, a summer resident fascinated with archaeology in the early part of the twentieth century.

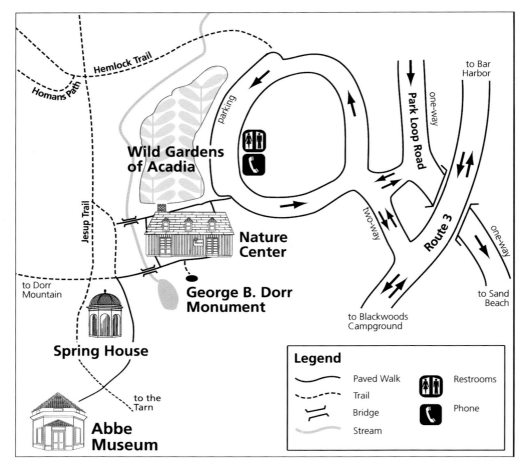

National Park Service

GEORGE DORR

George Bucknam Dorr never paid much attention to his bank account. Inheritor of vast fortunes from both sides of his family – a total estimated to be about $10 million dollars then; the equivalent of $230 million now – he just assumed there would always be enough to pursue his interests. Highest among those was the conservation of his beloved Mount Desert Island.

The Dorr family was part of the first wave of summer residents on the island, having built the second cottage on MDI in 1868. Educated at Harvard and Oxford, George Dorr was a lover of the outdoors and a student of landscape gardening, even opening a nursery on Mount Desert Island. Like Charles Eliot, John S. Kennedy, George Vanderbilt, and many others, Dorr became concerned when the portable sawmill appeared on the island. It looked like it could eat whole hillsides. In 1901, Dorr attended a meeting between the village improvement societies of Seal, Northeast, and Bar Harbors to look into preserving land for public use. The effort would result in Acadia, the first national park created from donated lands.

Dorr used up his entire fortune buying acreage for preservation, donating Sieur de Monts and countless other places. When he became director of Sieur de Monts National Monument in 1916, the tireless Dorr took no salary. But when he became the first superintendent of Acadia National Park he did agree to a salary – because he had no money left. He remained in the position until his death in 1944.

EGG ROCK LIGHT

Egg Rock Light has been protecting sailors for more than a century, blinking once every five seconds to alert seafarers to the dangers at the mouth of Frenchman Bay. The island it sits on was named Egg Rock, not because it has saved many ships from scrambling their hulls on its granite foundation, but because collectors used to gather seabird eggs out on the lonely isle. In the nineteenth century egg collecting was a popular hobby – there are many Egg Rocks along the Maine coast - and people would row the four miles out from Bar Harbor to fill their bags with puffin and great auk eggs. Between these egg collectors and people taking birds for their feathers, the population of many seabirds was decimated. The great auk went extinct, but the puffin has been saved by the crusading work of the Audubon Society, and colonies of the clown-faced birds now dot the Maine coast.

Construction of the light in 1875 was prompted by the growing popularity of Bar Harbor at the end of the

nineteenth century. Increasing boat traffic meant increased risk of shipwrecks. And plenty of ships have gone aground here thanks to frequent banks of fog, so thick it's more like stew than soup. These low-lying clouds are created when the cold waters of the Gulf of Maine meet the warm air off the land. The chilly water cools the air, lowering its dew point and causing condensation. The result is some of the thickest fog in the nation.

Egg Rock Lighthouse is located in the entrance to Frenchman Bay.

The cannon pictured in this photo is now located near the waterfront in Bar Harbor.

BASS HARBOR LIGHT

Standing guard at the southernmost tip of Mount Desert Island, Bass Harbor Light is one of five beacons protecting Acadia National Park, and it's one of the most photographed lighthouses in Maine. The thirty-two-foot tower was built in 1858, and it's one of the few lighthouses on the Maine coast that's easily visited by the public, sitting high on a cliff looking out over an archipelago of islands.

Bass Harbor Light ————

A series of switchbacks takes hikers up the facade of Champlain Mountain along the Precipice Trail.

4 ladders and 183 iron rungs were fixed to the side of Champlain Mountain to assist hikers on the Precipice Trail.

THE PRECIPICE TRAIL

Many hikers consider the Precipice Trail *the* trail for adventure in Acadia National Park. Why? Because, just as it's name suggests, it goes right up the face of a 1,000-foot cliff. Using a series of 252 steps, 4 ladders, and a total of 183 iron rungs, the "trail" hangs off the side of Champlain Mountain, and it's not for those afraid of heights. It's open and exposed nearly the entire way up.

The impressive East face of Champlain Mountain has captivated people since the first adventurers arrived in Bar Harbor in the mid nineteenth century. No one thought it was climbable, however, until a Princeton language professor named Rudolph Brunnow showed it could be done. He did a free ascent in the late nineteenth century and fell in love with it, returning in 1912 to construct a trail so that everyone could share the experience.

Opened in 1915, the Precipice was an immediate hit. Back in Washington, the bosses of the National Park Service were impressed, saying, "We know of no other trail so nobly built as this. Many flights of huge granite steps make possible, to all ascents which none but the daring would otherwise take, and yet the impression of undisturbed nature remains."

PEREGRINE FALCON
Falco peregrinus

In 1970, there were fewer than forty nesting pairs of peregrine falcons in the entire lower 48. Fast and furious fliers, the peregrine can hit speeds of more than 100 mph as it dives on its prey. Yet, the powerful birds were very sensitive to pesticides, which thinned the eggs of their young, making it all but impossible for them to reproduce. Acadia was one of several sites included in a restoration program begun in the 1980s. Today dozens of chicks have been hatched on Mount Desert Island, many of them right off the Precipice Trail.

Peregrine falcon silhouette

Viewing peregrine falcons is a popular activity in the spring and early summer at Champlain Mountain.

SCHOONER HEAD

Two competing legends from an 1885 Bar Harbor Herald newspaper article vie for the naming rights of Schooner Head. One legend claims that during the War of 1812 the captain of a British frigate mistook the headlands for a Yankee Schooner and let loose with his cannons. The other legend claims the name is derived from none other than the pirate Captain Kidd, who supposedly liked to hide on Mount Desert Island. It's said he was being chased by a British

man-of-war, and planned to seek cover in Otter Cove. A fog swept in, however, and he ended up smashing into this rocky headland, where some say his ghost walks to this day.

Private Residence

Schooner Head

Frenchman Bay

SAND BEACH

On a sunny summer day, you can hardly see the sands of Sand Beach - they're covered by towels and beach blankets. This is Acadia's only sandy beach. Consequently it's one of the most popular places in the park, despite the fact that the water rarely gets above 55-60 degrees. In a state famous for its rockbound coast, Sand Beach is an anomaly. You won't find another wide-open stretch of fine saltwater sands for many miles in either direction. That's because Sand Beach is a pocket beach. Nestled in a cove between Great Head on one side and the cliffs of Ocean Drive on the other, the beach is partially protected from the pounding surf of the ocean. The relatively quiet waters and gentle slope allow the beach to hold onto the fine sediments — and little creatures - that are swept in here.

Sand Beach

Up to seventy percent of its sands are from the crushed bodies of barnacles and mussels and urchins - more biogenic content than any other beach in Maine. It also has more sand per yard than any other beach north of Pemaquid. Some years, when the sands shift with extreme high tides and rough weather, you can see the remaining ribs of the schooner Tay, a windjammer that ran aground on Old Soaker in 1911 and was buried here.

In 1910, the illustrious banker J.P. Morgan bought the entire beach as a gift for his daughter and her husband. Almost forty years later, his granddaughter donated the beach and adjacent lands to the park.

J. P. MORGAN BUYS 'BEACH SITE

Purchases 117 Acres at Great Head for His Daughter, Mrs. Satterlee.

Special to The New York Times.

BAR HARBOR, Me., Aug. 19.—The tract of land at Great Head, consisting of 117 acres, which includes the famous sand beach property, has been purchased by J. Pierpont Morgan for his daughter, Mrs. Herbert L. Satterlee of New York. Mr. Morgan is here now on his yacht Corsair looking over his newly acquired property, and Mr. and Mrs. Satterlee, who will come shortly, will build a cottage.

The property was originally owned by the heirs of Frances McCauley and Sara Stratton, and about a year ago a lawsuit took place between their heirs and the heirs of William Bingham, one of the earlier owners of the land.

The New York Times
Published: August 20, 1910
Copyright © The New York Times

Great Head Trail

Newport Cove

Old Soaker

View of Sand Beach from the Ocean Path trail

OCEAN PATH TRAIL

One of the easiest walks in Acadia, the Ocean Path Trail is also among the most rewarding. The trail covers about two miles between Sand Beach and Otter Point, paralleling Ocean Drive. The flat gravel pathway follows the course of an old buckboard road that took the earliest of Acadia's visitors along the shore. The trail was a project of the Civilian Conservation Corps in the 1930s, and the first 7,000 feet took them 5,000 man-days to complete. John D. Rockefeller Jr. thought the new path should extend all the way to Otter Cliffs and financed the second half of the building effort.

Gorham M

Otter Point

GLACIAL PLUCKING

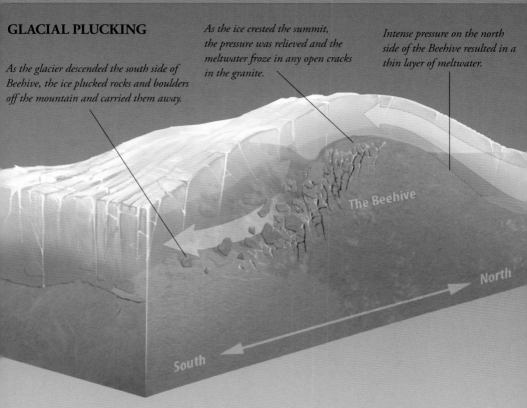

As the glacier descended the south side of Beehive, the ice plucked rocks and boulders off the mountain and carried them away.

As the ice crested the summit, the pressure was relieved and the meltwater froze in any open cracks in the granite.

Intense pressure on the north side of the Beehive resulted in a thin layer of meltwater.

The Beehive

North

South

When the last glaciers advanced southward through Acadia, the ice ran into the granite ridge that ran east-west across the island. Here at the Beehive, the ice was forced upward over the ridge. The resulting pressure caused the ice to ride on a thin layer of water. When the glacier crested the top of the ridge, the pressure was relieved and the water froze like fingers in the cracks and crevices of the rock. As the glacier continued its journey, the ice fingers plucked chunks of rock from the south side of the mountain and carried them away. The resulting shape is a classic example of what geologists call *roches moutonnees* or sheep back mountains. The gradual northern slope and steeper southern slope give the appearance of a sheep grazing with its head down. Several other mountains in the park (e.g. South Bubble) also display this telltale sign of glacial plucking.

The Beehive

Sand Beach

🚶 *Ocean Path Trail*

🚶 *Beehive Trail*

THE BEEHIVE TRAIL

Switching back and forth up the broken face of a cliff, the Beehive Trail is second only to the Precipice at Acadia for non-technical thrills and chills. Visitors to Sand beach often look up to watch climbers on their way up the path, which rises 520 exhilarating feet to look out across the ocean. Scaling the Beehive requires 47 steps, 21 rungs, 2 bridges – and a lot of courage.

Great Head

Sand Beach

Great Head Trail

The view of Sand Beach from the Beehive Trail

THUNDER HOLE

Crowds have been lining up to hear the famous boom of Thunder Hole for more than a hundred years. When the conditions are right, a surge of water forces air into the narrow cavern, trapping it inside a sea cave at the back of the channel. If it's hitting hard enough, the compressed air has the concussive force of artillery fire. But timing is everything at this Park Loop Road favorite. For many visitors Thunder Hole doesn't thunder at all, but gurgles and sloshes. Best time to catch the action is three hours into a rising tide or during a storm.

MONUMENT COVE

The twenty-foot tower of Monument Cove was caused, like so many other Acadia attractions, by erosion. Constant wave action slowly wore down weaker rocks, leaving behind this natural obelisk. The beach below it is a boulder beach, comprised of large chunks of rock that are being tumbled smooth by the waves. Monument Cove is viewable from above by walking the Ocean Path. There are no official trails accessing the cove itself.

OTTER CLIFFS

Despite the name Otter Cliffs, sea otters are not native to Maine. River otters are, but they are rarely seen today. More common at this 100-foot cliff of granite are tourists and rock climbers.

Local lore has it that Samuel de Champlain's ship was scuttled just offshore here when he sailed through the area in 1604. The French explorer was on his way to have a meeting with the Wabanakis when he struck the Spindle, a submerged rock just offshore, and was supposedly forced to limp into Otter Cove for repairs. The veracity of that story is debated, as there are many other locations along the Maine shore that fit the description, but Champlain certainly spent time exploring the shoreline here and is credited with naming the island.

A few hundred years later, this area was very popular with the cottage crowd. Summercators like Theodore Roosevelt and Charles Eliot would hike down and explore the shore. Affluent tourists visited so often in fact, that the enterprising owner of the land erected a gate and charged them ten cents for a look off the cliffs.

During the first World War, this area was the site of a naval radio tower that listened for offshore activity in the Gulf of Maine. The Mount Desert Island man who donated the land and oversaw the station – Alessandro

Otter Cliffs

The Spindle

Fabbri - was later given a Navy Cross for developing the "most important and most efficient station in the world." By the 1930s though, the station seemed at odds with the pretty Ocean Drive that was being developed here. John D. Rockefeller, Jr. offered the Navy an alternate site on Schoodic Peninsula and the station was moved.

Otter Cliffs is one of the most popular rock climbing destinations in Maine. The park allows teams of up to twelve to climb the wall and there are a couple of outfitters in Bar Harbor who offer guide services.

TIDEPOOLS & THE INTERTIDAL ZONE

Tidepools occur in the *intertidal zone*: a vertical stretch of shore located between the high and low tide levels. Rapidly changing levels of water, temperature, and oxygen in this zone support a variety of sea creatures adapted to tough conditions.

As the tide recedes, the first things you'll typically see are tiny white barnacles. Deeper in the pool you'll find stringy mats of greenish-brown rockweed, which often hide green crabs and periwinkles. Short, frilly red seaweed called Irish moss dominates the next section. The bottom level, which is rarely exposed to air, supports creatures like sea stars and urchins. If you're lucky, you might spy a sea anemone, a sponge or even a baby lobster.

HELP PROTECT THE PARK AND YOURSELF

Do not wade or sit in tidepools.

Rocks and algae are slippery. Watch your step.

Never turn your back on the ocean: rogue waves can occur at any time.

Wear suitable clothing and closed-toe shoes.

Sea creatures live everywhere. Be careful where you place your feet.

If you move animals or rocks, return them to the same spot.

Do not pry animals from rocks; you may injure them in the process.

Re-cover animals you find under rocks or seaweed so they won't dry out.

All living creatures are protected in the park. Take only pictures.

TIDES

The highest tides in the world wash in and out of the Gulf of Maine. Just northeast of Acadia, in the Bay of Fundy, the swing can be as much as 52 feet. At Acadia, the tides range from 8 to 12 feet.

What causes this endless ebb and flow? Gravity, mostly. The moon has enough gravitational pull to stretch the sea toward it, as it orbits the Earth. The sun, too, pulls at the ocean, but it is so much farther away that its gravity has less of an effect. The two celestial beings join forces during a full moon and a new moon, creating tides that are very high and very low. And sometimes they work against each other – during a quarter moon the sun and moon are at right angles and the one partially cancels the effect of the other. Scientists call these *neap* tides. They are characterized by dampened variations between high and low tide levels.

The centrifugal force of the Earth's rotation creates another bulge of water (high tide) on the opposite side of the Earth.

LOBSTER
Homerus Americanus

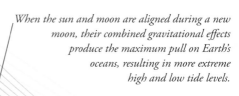

Lobster can be found as far south as North Carolina and as far north as Newfoundland. But everyone knows, Maine lobster is best. Maine fishermen caught 63 million pounds of lobster as of last count, a catch worth \$235 million dollars. Although Canada is the world's largest supplier of lobster, Maine brings in 62 percent of all the lobster caught in the U.S.

When the sun and moon are aligned during a new moon, their combined gravitational effects produce the maximum pull on Earth's oceans, resulting in more extreme high and low tide levels.

Low tide

LITTLE HUNTERS BEACH

Little Hunters Beach is made up of cobbles — rounded rocks between 2.5 and 10 inches in diameter — which click and clack as the waves wash over them. The rocks here were tumbled smooth by waves after falling out of the surrounding cliffs. Look closely and you may notice something strange. Some of the cobbles look like a geological version of chocolate chip cookie dough, with chunks of a darker rock mixed into lighter colored granite. It is evidence of something geologists call the *shatter zone*.

Millions of years ago, a plume of magma bubbled up from the Earth's core and worked its way toward the surface. The rising magma fractured and melted the bedrock above it. This shatter zone is characterized by the older rock that became encased in the edges of the magma. It surrounds the pink granite mountains of Acadia like a wide ring.

JORDAN POND

Jordan Pond was formed by a glacier approximately 12,000 years ago. As the ice advanced, it carved out the U-shaped valley between Pemetic Mountain and Penobscot Mountain where Jordan Pond sits today. When the climate warmed, the southern edge of the glacier began to recede, even while the interior portions of the glacier continued to advance. Acting like a conveyor belt, the ice deposited accumulations of rock, gravel, and sand at its melting edge. At the southern end of the valley, a large pile of this debris, technically called a *moraine*, formed a natural dam. The moraine trapped the water as the glacier receded, forming a lake 150 feet deep, the deepest on the island. Today, the Jordan Pond House sits atop that moraine. You can still see evidence of the glacial boulders and sediments at the southern end of Jordan Pond.

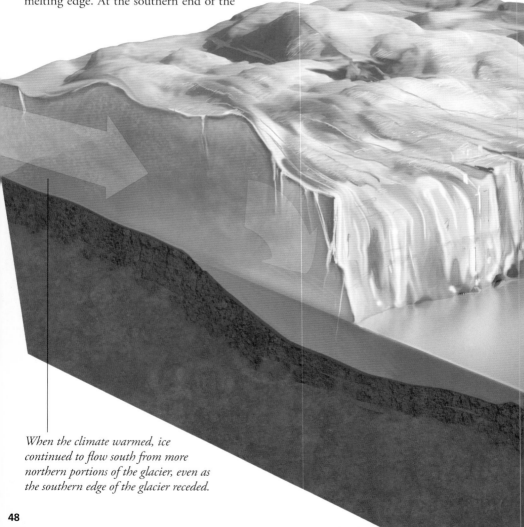

When the climate warmed, ice continued to flow south from more northern portions of the glacier, even as the southern edge of the glacier receded.

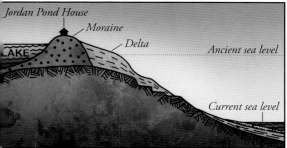

Before the land rebounded from the weight of the glacier, the ocean stretched inland to a delta that formed south of the Jordan Pond moraine. When the land began to rise, the delta was lifted out of the ocean and the coastline receded.

Source: Adapted from Maine Geological Survey

When the valley filled with meltwater, Jordan Pond was created.

As the glacier receded, it left behind a pile of debris called a moraine that dammed the valley.

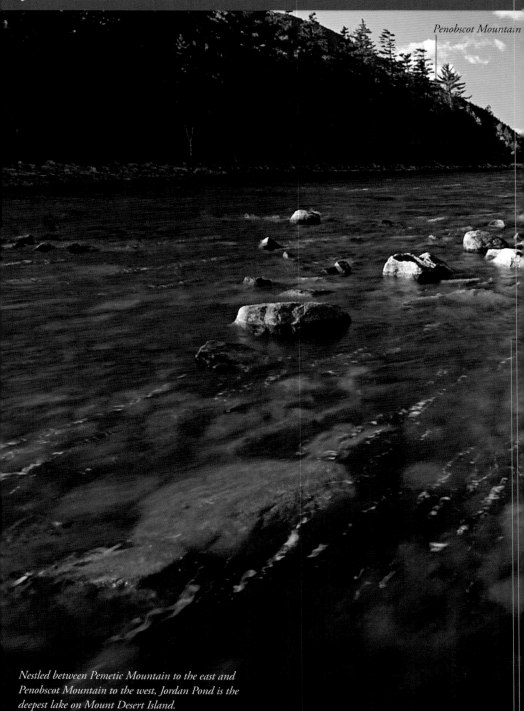

Penobscot Mountain

Nestled between Pemetic Mountain to the east and Penobscot Mountain to the west, Jordan Pond is the deepest lake on Mount Desert Island.

Pemetic Mountain

South Bubble

North Bubble

BUBBLE ROCK

Bubble Rock is a fourteen ton boulder sitting high on the side of South Bubble Mountain. Its original home was approximately 20 miles to the northwest. Geologists know this because Bubble Rock is composed of a type of granite that is different than the pink granite found here in Acadia. The technical term for this kind of misplaced boulder is a *glacial erratic*.

Glacial erratics are boulders that are picked up by advancing glaciers and deposited in new locations. Geologists believe Bubble Rock started off somewhere near Lucerne, a small town on the way to Bangor, where a similar

Bubble Rock

Eagle Lake

type of granite is found. When the glaciers melted, Bubble Rock was left perched on the side of the mountain.

Pemetic Mountain

adillac Mountain

POPOVERS AND TEA

For more than a century, Jordan Pond has a been a getaway for island visitors looking for a bit of quiet and serenity after all the activity at the shore. Surrounded by peaks, its placid waters have attracted explorers, artists, and fishermen since the mid-nineteenth century. In the 1870s, the farmer who owned the pond got the idea that he could make some money off all of these guests and began to serve lunch. When new owners purchased the property, they decided to make things more formal, opening the Jordan Pond House in 1896. They too offered lunch and became famous for their tea and popovers. The tradition of popovers at the pond persisted and prospered until 1979, when a fire burned the original Jordan Pond House. Private funds helped rebuild the structure and it continues to be popular today. So much so that it's a good idea to call ahead for reservations.

Visitors enjoying lunch at the Jordan Pond House

*John D. Rockefeller, Jr.
and his father, the founder
of Standard Oil*

JOHN D. ROCKEFELLER, JR.

John D. Rockefeller, Jr. inherited a lot from his father. John D. Rockefeller, Sr. was a founder of Standard Oil and reaped the profits of the early oil explosion – some called him the richest man ever - leaving his son billions in today's dollars. But he passed on another gift – a love of road building. JDR, Sr. built carriage roads on his New York and Ohio estates. And he also taught his son the importance of philanthropy. All of these inheritances – money and road construction and a willingness to help – would profoundly impact Acadia National Park.

"Junior" as he was known, graduated from Brown University and became a Standard Oil director. He first came to Mount Desert Island in 1908 and like so many others, fell in love with the place. When the preservation movement that would result in Acadia began, he got involved. A fan of national parks - he contributed to the Grand Tetons, Great Smoky Mountains, Yosemite and Shenandoah. He eventually donated more than $3.5 million dollars and 11,000 acres to Acadia.

Rockefeller will forever be known as the creator of the park's carriage roads. Today over 57 miles of these genteel gravel byways wander through the interior of Acadia, beloved by horsemen, bikers, and hikers alike. "Mr. Rockefeller's Roads" were state of the art at the time, and remain the best example of broken stone roads in the country. Building the carriage paths took twenty-seven years, and Rockefeller oversaw the whole process, hiring some of the nation's best architects and engineers, walking the roads, checking the gradients, and planning the landscaping. All because he preferred horses and carriages to automobiles.

Carriage road gate house

Carriage Roads

YOU ARE HERE

Over 57 miles of carriage roads wind their way through the park

No two of Acadia's seventeen carriage road bridges are alike.

EAGLE LAKE

Eagle Lake got its name from painter Thomas Cole, who looked up one day while at his easel to see one of the great raptors flying overhead.

At 110 feet deep, Eagle Lake is the third deepest lake on the island and is stocked with togue, landlocked salmon, and brook trout. Fishing is allowed with a permit, but it's clean waters are the source of Bar Harbor's drinking water, so no swimming is permitted.

In the late 1800s, the steamship Wauwinnett used to ferry passengers to the base of Cadillac Mountain where they could ride a cog railway to the summit. The ship eventually sunk and now lies at the bottom of the lake.

View of Eagle Lake (foreground) from Cadillac Mountain

BALD EAGLE
Haliaeetus leucocephalus

The "white-headed sea eagle," *Haliaeetus leucocephalus*, is the largest bird of prey in North America. Their nests are equally impressive, reaching weights of more than one ton.

Wingspan can reach greater than 7 feet

Juvenile bald eagles have brown head feathers

Yellow iris

Hooked bill for tearing flesh

White tail feathers

The bald eagle immobilizes its prey with its front talons, while it pierces flesh and organs with the rear talon

White head with distinctive mask feathers that reach around the neck

Closable nostrils allow osprey to keep water out when they dive after fish

OSPREY
Pandion haliaetus

The osprey is popularly known as the sea hawk. Special adaptations make it particularly suited for catching fish – its primary food source.

Wingspan can reach six feet

The Osprey's outer toe is reversible, allowing it to hold its prey with two toes in front and behind

SUNRISE ON CADILLAC

When the sun rises in the morning, Cadillac Mountain is the first place in the United States that it smiles upon – at least for part of the year. Sunrise on Cadillac is a Maine tradition and a lot of people like to greet the dawn here.

Maine is America's easternmost state and Cadillac Mountain is the tallest point within twenty-five miles of the Atlantic coast all the way south to Rio de Janeiro. That combination of height and longitude means that Cadillac gets

Burnt Porcupine Island

Sheep Porcupine Island

Long Porcupine Island

Frenchman Bay

Bald Porcupine Island

Lead Mountain

Jordan Island

to see the first rays of morning light between March and October. During the rest of the year, tiny Mars Hill, in Aroostook County, Maine, lays its claim to the dawn. Some have said that Mount Katahdin, because it's the highest peak in Maine, is the place where the United States greets the day, but the U.S. Naval Observatory did a study at the new millennium, confirming Cadillac's rightful place in the pecking order.

Ironbound Island

Winter Harbor

Turtle Island

Egg Rock

Schoodic Head

Schoodic Point

Gulf of Maine

A typical dawn scene on top of Cadillac Mountain

CADILLAC'S NAME

Originally called Green Mountain, this peak's name was changed to Cadillac Mountain in 1918 by George Dorr, the park's first superintendent. Dorr named it after a Frenchman with a colorful history, Antoine Laumet.

Antoine came to the new world in 1688. Some believe he was fleeing France. Whether or not that's the case, one thing is for certain: Antione assumed a new identity shortly after his arrival. He invented a bogus noble title, "Sieur de la Mothe Cadillac" and even contrived his own coat of arms (upper right).

Antoine's gamble on a new persona paid off. Shortly after reinventing himself, he secured a land grant from the French crown that included Mount Desert Island. He didn't stay long, however. Cadillac moved west where he went on to found the city of Detroit, the eventual car capital of America.

In 1902, around the time of the city's bicentennial, a new car company was born from the remains of a failed business of Henry T. Ford. The new owners decided to pay tribute to the city's founder, naming the company Cadillac Automobile Company. They even adopted a modernized version of his coat of arms (lower right) that adorns the hoods of their cars.

La Mothe Cadillac's coat of arms

Cadillac automobile symbol

Park ranger leading a talk on Cadillac Mountain

GREEN MOUNTAIN HOTEL & RAILWAY

When captains of industry discovered the island in the late 19th century, hiking or "tramping" was a favorite activity. Of course, in those days rich summercators didn't want to go anywhere they couldn't get a cup of tea, so a hotel was built atop the mountain where 50 guests could stay the night.

In the 1880s, tramping wasn't the only way to get to the summit. For many, the journey started with a carriage ride from Bar Harbor to Eagle Lake. There, they boarded the steamship *Wauwinnet* and took a 15-minute ride across the lake. Next, they climbed aboard the Green Mountain Cog Railway and a half-hour later were standing on the summit. Today most everyone arrives atop Cadillac by car, climbing the 3.5-mile Summit Road. Both the hotel and railroad had short lives, going out of business by the turn of the century.

The Green Mountain Hotel could accommodate 50 guests. It was eventually torn down in 1896

The railway went bankrupt in 1889. The train ended up in New Hampshire taking passengers up Mount Washington.

Green Mountain Railway ticket

PRODUCTION CREDITS
Written and narrated by Andrew Vietze

Edited by Laurie Olson

Graphic artist: Travis Commeau

Recording and sound design by Acadia Recording Company, Portland, Maine

www.acadiarecording.com

Driving instruction narration: Regina Bartholomew

PHOTOGRAPHY CREDITS
Photography by Paul Davis unless otherwise noted below

Sue Anne Hodges (www.sueannehodges.com): pages 15, 54-55, 58-59, 60-61, 66-67

Lisa Mossel Vietze: back cover (portrait of Andrew Vietze)

National Park Service: 16, 17, 21, 38, 68

Maine Historical Association / Jesup Memorial Library: 16

Historic American Engineering Record, National Park Service Harlen D. Groe, Ed Lupyak,
Sarah Desbiens, Joe Korzeniewski, and Neil Maher,1995: 57

Library of Congress: 10, 11, 13, 56, 57

iStockPhoto: 23, 27, 45, 63

ILLUSTRATION CREDITS
Charles Carter: 6, 7, 9, 33, 45, 48, 49

Gary Freeman: 44

Yellowstone Expedition Guide

Guidebook

Audio Tour

Computer CD-ROM

A COMPREHENSIVE GUIDE TO THE WONDERS OF YELLOWSTONE

SELF-GUIDED AUDIO TOUR

3D GEOLOGY DIAGRAMS

200-PAGE ILLUSTRATED GUIDEBOOK

GUIDE TO ANIMALS & PLANTS

GUIDE TO HIKING TRAILS

VIRTUAL YELLOWSTONE ON CD-ROM

WINNER
NATIONAL OUTDOOR
BOOK AWARD

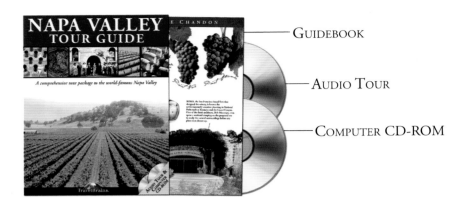

Guidebook

Audio Tour

Computer DVD-ROM

The Modern Way to Tour America's Historic Sites

GETTYSBURG

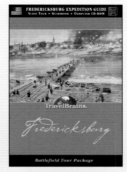

FREDERICKSBURG

VICKSBURG

2ND MANASSAS

GREAT BATTLES OF THE CIVIL WAR ANIMATED